DORRY

A Special Cor

Edited by Alan Vowles

Avon and Somerset Constabulary History and Heritage Group

This edition © Alan Vowles & Avon and Somerset Constabulary 2017

DORRY'S WAR

A Special Constable at war

Being the wartime memoirs of Joseph William Dorrinton in his own words

CONTENTS   PAGE

Foreword   9

Introduction   11

1. How it all started   17
2. The onset of war   23
3. Life on the beat   29
4. Baptism   36
5. Siren nights   40
6. Drunks and death   45
7. Blitz   59
8. The aftermath of bombing   64
9. New cars and tin hats   70
10. A long tour   78
11. UXB and W.A.P.C.   89
12. Afterthoughts   93
13. Looking back   97

APPENDICES

A – Letter from Dorry Dorrinton

Foreword by

SPECIAL CONSTABULARY CHIEF OFFICER DAVID FARRELL

On a crisp sunny afternoon in January 1994, I joined more than one thousand Special Constables from all forces across the UK and together we marched in uniform and solidarity to Coventry Cathedral; it was an impressive sight. I still vividly recall the sense of pride and comradeship that we all shared as we stepped in unison, led by the West Midlands Pipe Band.

The occasion was a Service of Dedication of a Book of Remembrance commemorating the names of 529 Specials, War Reserves, Parish Constables and RUC Reservists who had died on duty since 1801. Compiled by John Jones, Secretary of the National Association of Special Constabulary Officers, the list was the result of over two years of painstaking research. HRH the Princess Royal, and many dignitaries including Trefor Morris, HMIC Chief Inspector of Constabulary, Michael Winner, chair of the Police Memorial Trust and Brandon Moss, the Coventry City Special awarded the first George Cross in 1940, all attended the Service.

In his address the Rt. Rev. Clive Handford, Bishop of Warwick described the Book of Remembrance as a symbol of the "compassionate authority" that lies at the heart of all policing, but which is epitomized by the voluntary Special Constabulary.

I joined the Avon and Somerset Constabulary in 1984, as SC 1217, just six and a half years after Joseph "Dorry" Dorrinton had retired. I collected the same uniform that he was issued with (no steel helmet or respirator!) from the Bridewell, in Bristol and, with minimal training, joined regular colleagues in the world of policing on multiple duties each week. Over the intervening years, the role of Specials has changed almost beyond recognition. Patrol uniform is now body armour; while the equivalent of yesteryears "appointments" now includes incapacitant spray, body worn video camera, encrypted radios and smartphones with digital pocketbook as everyday tools. Structured learning endorsed by the College of Policing provides development opportunities ranging from initial training through supervisor development and onto senior leadership programmes. Specials are now deployed in a growing array of front line and specialist roles, once thought unthinkable. Every Special volunteer steps out from their "other life" into policing to contribute and participate in their local community. Each has a unique story to tell, Why do they join? How do they cope with on duty experiences? What keeps them coming back? How do they balance policing and external demands of work and family?

While their stories are different, the common theme of these citizens in uniform across the years, as with Dorry, is one of dedication to duty, complete selflessness and amazing resilience.

The Police Roll of Honour lists the names of two Specials in Somerset Constabulary, four in Bristol Constabulary and eight in Bath City Police who lost their lives in the line of duty between 1939 and 1945. For each of the last ten years as Chief Officer, I have placed a commemorative poppy wreath, on behalf of the Special Constabulary, at the Cenotaph in Bristol on Remembrance Day. Having gained some insight into the remarkable tales of Dorry's War, this year shall be all the more poignant.

Avon and Somerset Constabulary HQ

February 2018

INTRODUCTION BY ALAN VOWLES – FORCE HISTORIAN

In the autumn of 2017 I took a visit to the Bristol archives where Avon and Somerset Constabulary have historically deposited a large collection of documents for safekeeping. The purpose of the visit was simply to confirm what they held on our behalf.

In amongst the collection I came across a typed manuscript filed together with a collection of letters, all relating to a Special Constable who had served in the Bristol Constabulary throughout the war years. I knew immediately that the manuscript was a little 'gem' – a document of unique historical significance for its first-hand account of life as a police officer during the 'Battle of Bristol'.

With copies in hand I set about reading the document and became so engrossed that I read the lot in a single sitting.

Joseph William Dorrington, known as 'Dorry' to everyone who knew him had sat at a typewriter and put the entire document together in early 1989. I was instantly caught up by the style of writing and the character of Dorry which shone through in his writings.

No, it is not a manuscript that will be held up as an example of grammar or punctuation but it is beautifully honest, to the point, informative and thought provoking. In the entire document, Dorry does not say a bad word about anyone, he doesn't criticise, complain or moan, he simply states the facts as he saw them during those terrible times.

As I read this story I gained a huge respect for this man, an Engineer by day and a Police Officer by night, who rose above the stress, the horror and the fatigue simply to do his duty. He did not write his manuscript for praise or reward, he had written it so that no one would forget the impact the Special Constabulary had in keeping the people of Bristol – and indeed the country – safe.

Dorry posted the document to the Chief Constable in 1989 with a covering note permitting the force to do with the document as they saw fit and it was this document that gave me the idea to publish the book in Dorry's name. Sadly, Dorry passed away several months after posting the book to the force and so he never had the chance to see any of it published. I hope that this belated publication, 29 years later will be adequate compensation.

One of the most endearing aspects of the book is the humour. It is very dry, very 'of its time' and very charming. Indeed, there is so much humour in the book that at one point it was considered to add cartoons. In the end I felt it better to publish it just as Dorry intended.

Therefore, the book you are about to read is entirely in Dorry's own words. I have added notes occasionally to explain a term he used that may not be familiar and on occasion have substituted a word or two to aid comprehension, but this book is as Dorry intended it. You will probably find that you are often left wanting more after reading parts of this, just as I was. It peaks your interest, raises questions and leaves you with a need to find out more.

As part of the publication process I took some time to look into Dorry's story a bit more.

He was born on 27 May 1916 and passed away 12 September 1989. For 39 years of his 73 years on earth he was a volunteer with the Special Constabulary and there are many ex 'Specials' and 'Regulars' around today who still remember him fondly. Most anecdotes seem to revolve around Dorry ferrying specials around in a battered old Volvo (something that you will see started in the war years). Other anecdotes relate to holidays people took with him and his family. Everyone has nothing but nice things to say about him and what better epitaph can there be.

The most striking thing that comes across to me in the entire book is the work ethic of Dorry and his colleagues. The high volume of hours they were working combined with the stress of the wartime police role and all this in addition to their 'day job' and family is astounding!

The History and Heritage group strive to record and remember every officer who has served in Avon and Somerset Constabulary and its constituent constabularies, this book is a natural addition to the collection.

I hope that as much as I did that you enjoy Dorry's War.

Alan

"This was the last scene, in the last act, in a drama that lasted almost four years.

Set in a wounded city which had bravely lived up to a proud and distinguished past, its players, humble citizens whose gallantry and fortitude will be an example for all time"

Joseph William Dorrinton 1989

How it all Started

"It all started in 1939, in February of that year to be precise. The war clouds were gathering and it seems more than likely that before long war would break out.

People began to look and see what they could do to help the war effort if it should come, and at that time, I was an engineer working at a power station working for the Bristol Corporation Electricity Dept.

I wondered what I could do that would give some use to my engineering skill, and I thought the Fire Brigade would possibly be an appropriate place.

I went down to Fire HQ and applied to join the Auxiliary Fire Service, only to be told that at the age of 22 I was too young. Therefore, I went around the corner to Police HQ with a view to joining the Special Constabulary[1].

I got the necessary application form, filled it out, and in due course after enquiries had been made, I was told that my application had been accepted.

Towards the end of March, I started training and we had to go for three nights a week for a period of about three hours each night. I was allocated to East Street Police Station,

Bedminster, the HQ of B Division, where I continued to serve until it closed in 1973.

Our training was divided into three parts, namely law, civil defence, and police duties.

The first part consisted of an outline of the various types of crime, of the offences of which we were most likely to come into contact and most important of all, the powers of arrest possessed by a police officer.

The second part consisted of lectures on how to recognize various types of bombs, how to deal with incendiary bombs[2], how to deal with a gas attack and we were given practice in the gas chamber of wearing our respirators in action. Practical lessons in how to put out fires using the stirrup pump were also given. We were then given details of the Civil Defence Organisation, how to fill up damage report forms and various items of a similar nature.

Police duties were perhaps the most detailed of the three parts.

First of all, we were taught how to fill up a notebook, marking the date, the time we reported for duty, the duty we were allocated to and anything that happened during that time.

In those days the Force was run on much more military lines than it is today[3]. We were taught how to parade for duty, we were given marching drill, and we were told how to salute and when to salute.

An officer above the rank of Sergeant was entitled to be saluted and had always to be addressed as Sir. A

Superintendent and above was entitled to a salute at all times whether he was in uniform or plain clothes.

If you failed to come to attention when addressed by an Inspector, to salute him and to address him as Sir, you would certainly get a reprimand before you went off duty.

The parade room at East Street Police Station was in a single storey building across the yard from the main block of offices.

When you reported for duty you went into the parade room and sat around until the sergeant came in, whereupon he told you to 'fall in' in two ranks and he detailed each officer with the duty that he was to perform during his tour.

The 'Beat' system was then in force and each man was given a particular beat to patrol, which consisted of a route laid down on a 'Beat Card' with very carefully timed appointments where the sergeant could expect to find you.

Naturally, if these were always worked in the same way the criminals would soon find out where the policeman was likely to be, so on some occasions you were told to work the beat backwards, or perhaps to start in the middle, go to the end, then go back to the beginning and work on until the middle.

Each beat lasted for about four hours and at the end of that time you were allowed to come in to the station for half an hour to have refreshments and were then allocated to another beat when you went back out.

You had to get to know all the premises on the beat and during the night tour you had to check all the fastenings on lock up premises to make sure that they were secure.

The only means of communication with the station was by means of police telephone pillars which were sited at strategic points, there being about 36 such pillars on the B Division.

In peacetime the HQ Station could flash a lamp on the top of the pillars to tell you that you were wanted and you then had to go to the pillar and answer it. During the war this was not possible due to the blackout, and therefore you had to report to a police pillar every time that you passed near to one.

When the sergeant had allocated the beats to each officer, he stood the parade at ease and went across to the Inspectors office to report that they were ready for inspection.

After a few minutes he came back followed by the Inspector, and as soon as he came into the Parade Room,

"Parade Attention".

In came the Inspector and gave the command,

"Produce your appointments."

You then had to stand with your gloves, pocket book, torch in your left hand and your truncheon in your right hand held up before you so the Inspector could see that you had all your equipment.

He then walked along the ranks inspecting uniform to see that it was tidy, to see that your boots were cleaned and your hair had been properly cut, just as you would do on a military parade.

When he was satisfied he gave the order,

"Return your appointments" and you put them away in their various pockets.

He then stood the parade at ease and proceeded to read The books were the daily information of crimes committed, other items of information and interest, messages received and recorded in the telephone message book, Daily Orders, Local Orders, transfers, resignations, new appointments and most peculiar of all, offences under the discipline code.

It was quite common to hear read out,

"Constable Jones, 26A has been fined a sum of five shillings for a period of four weeks for an offence against the Discipline Code, namely late on parade."

I can only assume that these offences were read out as an example to encourage the others!

After he had finished reading the books, he brought the parade to attention, right turn, quick march and one marched out of the Parade Room across the yard to the rear gate of the station and so into the street.

At the end of a tour of duty, one returned to the Parade Room and then the Sergeant checked off that everybody was back, if anyone had not arrived and the reason was not known, the parade would not be dismissed until he had been located and everyone was sure that all was well.

On day duties there were other things to be done, such as traffic points and various enquiries of people about offences they might have committed.

One point which had to be manned at all times day and night was at the bottom of the incline leading to Temple Meads Station. The Railway Police had jurisdiction only on their property and if anyone were arrested on the station for any offence such as theft, they had to be brought to the bottom of the incline and there handed over to the City Police who took them into custody.

After war had broken out, a further duty was added to the list namely the guarding of what were called vulnerable points, Waterworks, Power Stations, Gas Works, Telephone Exchanges, and places of similar importance. These also had to be guarded day and night as far as was possible in the light of manpower position.

[1] *At this time Fire HQ was Bridewell, Bristol as was the Police HQ.*
[2] *An amusing example of the incendiary technique being used can be found in the book 'When The Whistle Stops' by the History & Heritage Group.*
[3] *'Today' refers to approximately 1989.*

THE ONSET OF WAR

In May of that year I was sworn in as a Special Constable under Alderman Mr. Talbot Plum, J.P. and also took the oath under the Official Secrets Act, thus becoming a duly authorised officer of H.M. and the Law.

One day in August I took my mother to visit some friends of hers in Greville Road, Ashton and spend the evening there.

Suddenly there was a knock at the door and when it was answered, lo and behold there was a police constable outside. He asked if Mr. Dorrinton were there, and was told I was.

I went to the door and he immediately told me that we had been mobilized, that I was to go at once to East Street Police Station with my car, in order to commence duties.

When I arrived there *(The East Street station)* I was given the addresses of three other Special Constables, told to go to their houses, pick them up and take them to Central Police Station to be kitted out with uniform.

Upon arrival, we were each allocated a number, mine being SC700B which number I retained until after amalgamation with the Avon and Somerset Constabulary in 1974.

We were all issued with a tunic, trousers, leggings, greatcoat, gloves, raincoat and a cap with a waterproof cover. Also we had a whistle, truncheon, pocket book, steel helmet and service-type respirator.

Unfortunately, the uniform contractors had made a mistake with my uniform and I was not able to obtain it at that time.

Special Constables have never received any payment for doing their duties, it being a purely volunteer service, but we were then told as we were mobilized on a war footing that we should in future be entitled to claim travelling expenses to and from duty. We would also be eligible to claim a boot allowance of one shilling per week providing we did some duty and entitled to have a refreshment allowance which I believe at that time was one shilling for a four hour duty or one shilling and sixpence for eight hours.

We were not given any specific duties then but were expected to continue our training as we had been doing in the past.

Towards the end of August, however, there was one night when an experimental blackout was carried out and all Special Constables were called in to walk around the streets and make sure that people observed the blackout regulations.

On Sunday September 3 1939, I was on day shift in charge of the Avonmouth Rotary Sub-Station of the Electricity Dept. and I heard the fateful message from the Prime Minister that we were at war with Germany.

On the next evening that we reported for training, we were told that this would be the last training session and in future, we should be expected to do street duty. We were expected to do an average of 14 hours per week in turns of four hours each and also to report to our stations whenever the air raid sirens sounded if it were at all possible.

Although it is a long time ago now, I can well remember the first time I went on duty.

I paraded at 10 o'clock in the morning of a nice bright September day and I was told to go to the Provident Hall, Prewett Street, which was then in use as an Army Recruiting Centre. I was there to join Police Constable 90B Hutchings by name who was on duty outside the Hall.

As I walked up Prewett Street, I saw ahead a most imposing figure in dark blue uniform. He was well over six feet tall, as I approached him he looked down at me with a most friendly grin on his face and said,

"Hallo, young man, you've come out to learn how to be a policeman have you?"

As we paced slowly up and down, he gave me much information and advice and I shall never forget his kindness to a young recruit in showing him the way to carry out his duties.

Before going on to relate my experience during air raids, I would like to say a word about the air raid warning system. During 1938, a system of warning the population of approaching air raids had been set up and sirens had been installed throughout the country.

I don't know how many there were in Bristol, but it was probably round the 30 – 40 mark. These sirens could be operated from a central position and had also stand-by facilities for local operation, in case of breakdown.

The warning signal was given by switching the sirens on and off repeatedly to give a warbling note for about one minute. Similarly the All Clear was given by a steady continuous note for the same length of time.

Further, all important organisations like the railways, the police, fire stations, public utilities and large factories were equipped with one telephone line which was called the Air Raid Warning Line and had not to be used for any other purpose whatsoever.

Messages were sent over these lines, from the Central telephone Exchange and subscribers were allowed a period of five seconds to answer the telephone call. If it were not answered the call was cancelled and the exchange moved on to the next subscriber. Also a report was sent in to the organisation reporting that the telephone call had not been answered and enquiries were made.

Originally, there were four messages sent over these lines, the first one being Air Raid Message Yellow, which meant that enemy aircraft had crossed the coast from the continent, and that an air raid somewhere in the country was to be expected.

Some industries such as railways, docks, chemical works, power stations, gas works and the like had to have a certain amount of lighting during the hours of darkness in order that they could carry on with their work. When the Yellow message was received all this lighting had to be entirely extinguished and this caused considerable loss of production.

Although the message was not passed on to the public at that time, it did warn all organisations concerned with air raid precautions to stand-by in the anticipation of going into action.

The next message was Air Raid Warning Red, when this was received the sirens were sounded to notify the public that an air raid was expected in that area and they then went to their shelters.

After the enemy aircraft had passed, Air Raid Message Green was sent out and the sirens were sounded to give the All Clear. This enabled people to come out from their shelters and work in factories etc. to be resumed.

The last message was Air Raid Message White which meant that there were no aircraft over the country and that therefore external lighting could be put on and things returned to normal as far as possible.

As I have previously said, the Yellow Message was sent out whenever enemy aircraft were active over the country although it usually became obvious that no raid was intended in particular local areas. Sometimes the Yellow Message would be in operation for hours at an end, without any real need, and this caused considerable loss of production in certain factories etc.

It was, therefore, eventually decided to introduce a fifth message between yellow and red, and it was then laid down that on the receipt of Yellow (*Message*) external lighting need not be extinguished until the new message Air Raid Message Purple was received.

This was usually sent out when it appeared likely that a raid would take place in certain areas, and then the sirens would usually follow shortly after.

LIFE ON THE BEAT

My uniform arrived towards the end of September and I was then able to do full duties on the streets.

In common with about half a dozen Special Constables, I was approved to use my car on police duty and took my turn on a rota with them.

My shift duties at the Avonmouth Electricity Sub-Station were based on a four week cycle, and we used to have the day divided into three shifts, nine in the morning to three in the afternoon, three until ten in the evening and a long night shift from ten in the evening until nine in the following morning. Of course we also had days off from time to time.

As I lived some three miles from East Street Police Station, it was easier for me to do my duty in eight hour shifts rather than just four hours at a time, which was the longest period that any Special Constables could manage in view of the working during the day. I usually used to work for the police from ten in the evening until six in the morning or when I was on night shift at the power station I would come on police duty at ten in the morning until six in the evening.[1]

At that time B Division comprised the whole of the area within the City and County of Bristol lying to the south of a line running from Cumberland Basin along the floating harbor to the Feeder Canal out of St. Anne's and then along the river to the city boundary.

During the day time we used to be sent usually to do point duty, the common ones being Bristol Bridge South, Temple Gate and Ashton Gate where the Winterstoke Road and Ashton Avenue crossed the Weston-super-Mare road. This was particularly busy at weekends.

At night we used to patrol the streets doing ordinary police duties looking for insecure premises, trying to catch thieves etc. and also detecting and reporting offences against the black-out regulations when lights were shown from buildings accidentally or through carelessness.

There was not a great deal of road traffic in the evening as driving after dark was not at all pleasant. Motor vehicles were only allowed to display very limited lights. Their sidelights and rear lights having to be shown only through a space not more than one inch in diameter, and even that area had to be screened by tissue paper or similar substances behind the glass.

All headlights had to be fitted with masks, which only allowed light to come out through a small horizontal slit about half an inch wide and three to four inches long. Just above the slit was fixed a screen which prevented any light from being shown in an upward direction. As can be well imagined the light given for one to drive by was very very small, and as there were of course no street lights we were often kept very busy dealing with minor accidents.

Another duty which applied day or night, was the guarding of vulnerable points, the most important ones in B Division being Temple Back Power Station (my own place of work) and Rownham Water Tower.

At the bottom of Rownham Hill the water mains from Barrow reservoirs, to Victoria Pumping Station, Clifton, passed through a tunnel beneath the river, and on the river bank was a tower which gave access down into the tunnel. If a saboteur managed to damage these water mains it would have caused considerable disruption to life in the city.

Exactly what we were supposed to do if attacked we never found out, as, of course, we were unarmed and the nearest place where we could get assistance was the police pillar on Ashton Bridge about half a mile away.

Trams were then as yet in full operation in Bristol, and two routes in particular, namely, from Ashton Gate and Bedminster Down, terminated in Redcliffe Street just where it joined on to Victoria Street. The trams used to come into this terminus and then discharge their passengers in the middle of the road as usual. This was a very dangerous procedure after dark as the people getting off the trams could not very easily be seen by approaching motor cars, and a policeman was usually sent down there to stop the traffic while the tram discharged.

There were very many narrow escapes and it is remarkable that nobody was either killed or injured whilst getting off a tram there.

This comparatively peaceful existence lasted for the first nine months, and became known across the country as the Phoney War.

Before continuing with my reminiscences I would explain that although there are many incidents the date of which I know, there are many others that occurred where I am not at all certain exactly when it was, I will, however, endevour to give them in approximate order from start to finish.

Bristol Bridge South was not a very popular traffic point, owing to the manouvres performed by the trams there. There was a main route of trams which went up and down Victoria Street and across Bristol Bridge, but there was also another route which came from Temple Meads Station up Victoria Street and at Bristol Bridge turned right to go into Bath Street and so to Old Market.

In order to get round this corner into the rather narrow entrance of Bath Street, a tram coming from Victoria Street suddenly swung to the nearside of the road and then did a wide sweep across all the traffic into Bath Street and then disappeared.

Coming the other way trams coming out of Bath Street, did the same maneuver to the wrong side of Victoria Street and then turned down towards Temple Meads Station and rejoined their proper route.

One day I was on point duty there and had stopped the traffic coming up Victoria Street to allow traffic to come out from Bath Street and from Redcliffe Street.

My Inspector chose this particular moment to give me a visit. These visits, by the way, had to be recorded in one's pocket book by both the Constable and the Officer concerned with the time and place and then these could be cross-checked if necessary to make sure one was doing one's duty properly.

Anyway, suddenly I heard behind me Inspector Richardson[2] who had a very deep voice indeed and was extremely well spoken, suddenly this voice said,

"Hold that traffic in Victoria Street, 700."

Which of course I did and he then walked slowly across the intersection towards a motor car in the end of Victoria Street driven by a lady.

I noticed that this car had its left hand trafficator[3] sticking out indicating that she wanted to turn left and also the lady had her right arm out of the window indicating that she wanted to turn right.

Inspector Richardson walked very slowly and in a dignified manner up to the drivers window, he bent down and I heard him say,

"Excuse me, Madam, but did you know that your vehicle is about to divide in two?" I heard her exclamation of surprise and he continued to say,

"Yes it appears that the nearside of your vehicle is about to turn left whereas the offside is about to turn right. How the dickens can you expect my officer to know which way you want to go. Will you please ensure that in future you drive your vehicle in a proper manner."

One night during that cold winter, I reported for duty at East Street at 10 o'clock at night and was detailed for guard duty at Rownham Water Tower. Whenever possible two Special Constables were sent there at night in order to keep each other company and on this occasion I was lucky, I was sent down there with another Special.

Owing to the wintry and cold weather a sentry box had been put at the vulnerable point and a coke brazier had also been put there being screened with sheet iron so that no light from the fire could be seen.

It was the duty of everyone there to see that the fire was kept alight but unfortunately on this occasion the officers who had been down there on late turn had let the fire go out and when we arrived everything was stone cold.

At the back of the vulnerable point there was a ruined building, actually it was a house which had been a tea-gardens, a laundry, and all sorts of other things during its time and we had a look in there to see if we could find any materials to light the fire.

We found some bits of floorboard which had been pulled up and we took those out, and also we got some lino off the floor thinking this would catch fire easily and we should soon be warm again.

Unfortunately we did not realise how fast the lino would burn and suddenly flames shot out all over the place and lit up the Avon Gorge as though it were daylight. We had no means of putting the fire out and we just had to stand there hoping that the flames would soon die down.

Sure enough, they did, but not before they had been seen and we shortly had a visit from our Sergeant who wanted to know whether we'd seen any signs of fire down there. Of course we said,

"Oh no Sarge, we haven't seen anything," and luckily we managed to get away with it.

[1]It goes without saying that the hours Dorry was putting in were extraordinary. Working night shifts as an Engineer and then after only a couple of hours rest doing a full eight hours with the police before returning once more to night shift at his place of work. You certainly have to admire the work ethics of the war period.

[2]Basil Arthur Richardson. Ex Royal Navy with Bristol Constabulary long Service medal with 22 and 27 year bar, with the Defence Medal, British War Medal (WWI) and Victory Medal (WWI)

[3]The reader may be of a certain age that has not come across a 'trafficator'. These were early 'indicators' that popped up from the bodywork of a car to indicate its intention to turn in that direction. Normally metal in construction they were fitted with an orange reflective surface.

Baptism

As yet there had been no air raids actually in Bristol but the Yellow Message was very often received as either reconnaissance aircraft or bombers going further north in England passed over the city.

Scattered around the area were barrage balloon sites where there was a hut for the crew and a lorry fitted with a winch.

The barrage balloons were fabric envelopes, I am only guessing at the size, probably about 40 feet across and something like 90 feet long shaped like an airship[1]. These were filled with hydrogen and were secured to a wire cable which in turn was wrapped around the winch.

They could be flown at anything up to perhaps 5,000 feet and were used to discourage aircraft from coming in low.

Although no public warning was given when a Yellow message was received the public always knew when one was in operation as the barrage balloons were raised and flown on 'Yellow', being hauled down again when the 'White' was received.

One night when I was duty driver at East Street a message was received from a Warden's Post on Bedminster Down that someone in the Ashton Vale area was signaling to the enemy by means of light in morse code.

Detective Constable Freddie Wiltshire[2] and I were sent up to Bedminster Down to see what we could find.

Sure enough, when we got to the Warden's Post and looked down over the valley we could see a light flashing on and off just as though signals were being sent.

It took us about two hours to track this down and to find that the occupant of a house in the Ashton area had allowed light to creep around the side of his blackout curtains. This in turn was screened by a tree in front of the window whose branches were waving about in the breeze. This gave the appearance of signals being sent out in morse code and the occupant was severely reprimanded.

On 25 June 1940 this comparatively tranquil existence came to a sudden end.

I was in bed at home, sleeping the sleep of the just, when at 12.15 midnight I first heard the sirens sounding in anger. I got out of bed started to get into uniform and was almost completely dressed when the 'All Clear' sounded.

'Oh dear!' thought I, 'what a waste of time'.

So I started to undress again, but three minutes later the sirens sounded again giving a warning of a raid.

I got into my car and went down to East Street Police Station and reported for duty. As I was duty driving that night I didn't take the car out but parked it in the yard at the rear of the Station.

It was a nice bright moonlight night and regular Constable Phil Freeman[3] and I decided that we would best pass the time by sitting in the car and having a chat.

This we did and were thoroughly enjoying ourselves when at about half past one we heard the whistle of a descending bomb followed by a loud explosion.

Phil and I made one concerted dive out of the car on to the ground by the side and lay there until things went quiet. Within a few minutes the Sergeant came charging out of the main Police Station with two more Special Constables and said,

"Come on you three we're off to Brislington, a bomb has fallen in Edward Road."

Now as I have already said, it was very difficult driving the car at night, even with your headlights on, and we set off out of the back of East Street Police Station and then down York Road towards Temple Meads Station.

This of course was the first time that any real enemy action had taken place in the city, and the natives were somewhat nervous.

They certainly had strong objection to a car being driven during an air raid with its headlights on (although of course they were properly masked), so they started shouting and throwing stones at the car.

The Sergeant said,

"The best thing you can do Dorry is switch your lights off."

So I put the lights off. Of course then I couldn't see where I was going.

Luckily at that time I had a Morris Eight with a sunshine roof[4], so we pulled in to the side of the road and I decided the only thing to do was to slide the roof back. Therefore we set off again with the Sergeant standing on the passenger seat, the upper part of his body projecting through the roof so that he could see and tell me where to drive.

In this rather hazardous manner we eventually arrived at Edward Road to find that one house had been hit and demolished but fortunately no-one had been injured. Some reinforcements arrived soon afterwards and we left them to look after the incident while we returned to the Station.

At 02.35 hours the All Clear sounded and I went home to bed thus ending my first experience of real enemy activity.

[1]*Although there were a variety deployed, the most common barrage balloons were 57 feet in length with a diameter of 23 feet. So, not a bad guess!*
[2]*Police Constable 90 Frederick Edward Wiltshire, ex Lance Bombardier In the 127th Royal Garrison Artillery. Bristol Constabulary Long Service Medal with 22 and 27 year bar in addition to British War Medal and Victory Medal (WWI)*
[3]. *Philip Lunn Freeman,*
[4]*Small paneled sunroof in early cars.*

Siren Nights

This started the period that came to be known in Bristol as the period of siren nights.

Although there were not any heavy raids on Bristol it was a most tiring and wearying time as the sirens were continually sounding. In fact in the 127 days between the first raid on 25 June 1940 and 30 October 1940, the sirens sounded no less than 255 times, nearly twice a day.

Of course there were days when the sirens did not sound, but it was nothing unusual to have them go three or four times during the night and I seemed to spend most of my sleeping time driving to and from East Street to go on duty and come back again.

In this period I think one or two things must have happened.

One night I was down at Rownham Water Tower and got a visit from the Sergeant who really delighted me by saying,

"700, we've had a report of an aircraft having come down somewhere in the Avon Gorge. It might be on your ground, that is between the tow path and the river so you'd better go down and have a look. Take a walk to Pill and back and see if you can see anything."

You can imagine how delightful a trip it was in the middle of winter walking along the tow path by the river between Rownham and Pill with the only light to guide me being a torch and the tow path being very dilapidated and demolished in places. Never mind, I got there and back and of course, as expected, saw nothing.[1]

On the corner of Temple Way and Victoria Street was a huge building about two or three storeys high but they were very high storeys.

The building had been occupied before the war by the Henley Motor Co as a car showroom but they had now relocated and the building was used as a Forces canteen and dormitory where men in the Services could get a meal and a bed for the night. It was also open to Merchant Seamen but only on production of their pay book.

One night I was sent down there to see that no civilians had got in to use the canteen and it being a quiet night and no raid on, I got into the doorway and lit up my pipe.

I hadn't been there very long when a chap dressed in civilian clothes came up to the door and started to go in. As was my duty I said,

"Hey half a minute mate, you can't go in there."

"Oh" he replied, "Merchant Navy."

So I looked at his coat, couldn't see his badge showing that he was a member of the Merchant Navy, so I said,

"Right, let's see your Pay book."
"Oh, I haven't got it on me." He replied.
I said,
"I'm sorry you can't go in unless I see your pay book."
He gave me a hard look and said,
"You're smoking."
I said,
"Yes and what about it?"
He said
"I'll report you."
I said,
"OK, go ahead" and he replied
"Now can I go in?"
I said,
"Certainly not. You're trying to get me to let you in by threatening to report me for smoking." I continued, "Not on your life, go on, on your way." Off he went.

Two or three days later I went into East Street and reported for duty, and as I went up to the desk, the Sergeant looked over his spectacles and said,
"700, report to the Superintendent's Office."
I said "Right Sarge", went up and stood outside the Old Man's door wondering what the dickens was wrong this time.
I knocked on the door,
"Come in".
So I went in and came to attention in front of his desk with a brilliant salute,

"700 reporting as instructed Sir."

"Oh" he said, "just read this" throwing a piece of paper across his desk.

I picked it up and read it.

'*Mr Superintendent, do you know that one of your men 700 SC was smoking on duty outside the Forces Canteen in Victoria Street*' at such and such a time and such a date, and it was signed' '*A friend of Hitler.*'

Wally Hill who was the Superintendent looked up at me and said,

"Were you smoking?"

"Yes Sir."

"Well," he said, "you ruddy fool, next time you want to do it don't get caught. Go on get on duty."

And that was the end of that one.

However, I can well remember some amusing times at that canteen.

Later in the war when the Americans had joined us, it was of course open to American Servicemen. The Americans had a fair amount of absenteeism - and so did we I suppose - and they often used to raid the premises to see who was inside.

When one of these raids was occurring, squads were detailed at East Street, the American Police in their white helmets, usually known as snowdrops, our Naval Picket, the RAF Police, and our Military Police, the Redcaps. These would be all mixed together and round they would go in a couple of buses along to Victoria Street.

Once or twice when I was on duty there I had the privilege of seeing a raid carried out, and believe you me it was really funny.

They surrounded the building with a mixed force of various policemen and another squad went in, through the door to see who was inside and examine all the papers.

We used to see the Americans chewing their gum walking around the building swinging their night sticks - which were about three feet long - and suddenly the first floor windows would go up, figures would appear coming out through the windows, climbing over the sills with the Yankee M.P's standing down at the bottom and saying,

"Go on baby, I'se awaiting for you, come on down, I's right here."

Down they would come and usually they collected twenty or thirty absentees who were bundled into the vehicle and taken away to be interrogated.

[1] The village of Pill is approximately 4 miles by river from Rownham hill.

DRUNKS AND DEATH

On the 26 July 1940 the sirens were sounded for the forty-ninth time, giving their warning at 10.45 in the evening. I went down in my car to East Street as usual and went on 'stand-by' there.

It was, I remember a clear night but around midnight a summer thunderstorm started and then the fun began.

There were about 70 balloons being flown over the city at the time and they were soon being struck by lightning.

Altogether during that storm 28 balloons were destroyed before the authorities got round to instructing that they should be hauled down. Not only were these balloons destroyed but a lot of other damage was caused.

One case in particular was a balloon - probably anchored in the playground at the rear of Bristol South Baths - which was struck. The wind at that time was in a south westerly direction and the balloons were flying at an angle to the ground. As the balloon burnt and came down, its cable went across all the houses along the New Cut and eventually across the tramlines at Redcliffe Hill.

47

The balloon itself came down somewhere near Somerset square. The contact between the balloon cable and overhead wires of the trams caused any amount of sparking and damage and of course the balloon cable was lying across the houses for a distance of almost a mile.

The next morning there was extreme difficulty in recovering this cable without pulling the chimneys off too many houses and damaging their roofs.

These incidents taught the authorities a good lesson and in future no balloons were flown when there was thunder anywhere about.

One night in the Autumn of 1940 I paraded at East Street at ten o'clock and was given the duty of patrolling Victoria Street, that is from Bristol Bridge to Temple Gate. A regular constable, Jock Copeland[1] was given the job of mounting the guard at Temple Gate incline.

I went from East Street to Bristol Bridge and then commenced to Patrol Victoria Street on the right hand side going towards Temple Meads.

After some time, oh I expect it would be somewhere about midnight, I came down under the railway bridge near Temple Meads Station and saw the flash of Jock Copelands torch. I flashed back to him and went along and met round about Redcliffe Way now comes out into Temple Gate. He said to me,

"Have you seen anybody around here?" to which I replied,

"No, I haven't seen anyone Jock."

"Where the devil can he have got to? A funny little chap went past me just now walking towards you, you haven't seen him?" I answered,

"No, where the devil has he gone?"

"Ah", he said, "I know. I bet he's gone into the underground toilet near the Grosvenor Hotel, we'd better go and look."

One of our jobs at that time was to inspect all underground toilets, to see that nobody had been taken ill in there or was using them as a sleeping place. So down he and I went into the underground toilet banging on the doors. They were all open except one so Jock said,

"Och come on oot. Come on oot who's in there, come on oot I'll gie you five minutes."

We went back up the stairs and stood at the top and within two or three minutes, up the steps came a funny little bloke. He was about five foot nothing wearing a long overcoat, almost down to his ankles out of one pocket of which was sticking a bottle of whisky.

He came up pulling himself up by the handrail, obviously rather the worse for wear, we stopped him and asked him what he was doing and the usual sort of questions - where have you come from, where are you going. He didn't want to know, he didn't know anything.

We said, "What's your job?"

He said "A French polisher.

"Oh, how old are you?"

He said "82."

So Jock said, "When were you born?"

I can't do the mental arithmetic myself but the chap gave a date. Just to have a bit of fun with him Jock said,

"Oh you can't be, you can't be 82 if you were born in so and so."

The chap said, "Yes I was." Quite a well-spoken chap, "Oh yes I was."

Jock said, "You can't be man, that date doesn't tie up. It can't be the right date."

Well now, Jock was well over six feet and there was this little chap arguing with him about five feet I suppose, and Jock kept on really pulling his leg. I think the man appreciated it and he suddenly looks up, pointing his head straight up at the sky and said to Jock,

"You know, you want smartening up a bit."

So whereupon Jock felt he had had enough and said "Come on now on your way."

And off he goes up Victoria Street and into the darkness.

I stayed having a chat with Jock for a little while, and then I suppose, it would be then about half past one, I was due to go in for grub, no, it must have been a bit earlier about one o'clock, I was due to go for refreshment at half past one.

So I set off to walk to East Street, went in and had refreshments.

"What do I do second half Sarge?"

"Oh" he said, "You can take the same again. It'll keep you quiet."

Out I went along towards Bristol Bridge. This time I thought 'well, I'd better work down along the other side of Victoria Street', that is the left hand side going towards Temple Gate.

So I came along taking my steady way down and about half past two I suppose I came to the junction with Temple Way. As I have said before, Henley's Motor Company was on the far left hand corner of Temple Way. Next to the building was a hauling way which went back from Victoria Street about fifty yards or so in the open, closed off at the end by double doors. These in turn led into a part of the Henley Building which was used as an auxiliary Fire Station.

On the right hand of this hauling way as you stood with your back to Victoria Street, was a raised pavement which continued past the entrance to the Fire Station. In between the buildings was a narrow little footpath, it came out into Rose Street at the back.

Anyway, I walked down past Henley's building, past the hauling way, and I came opposite to this little footpath. As I walked slowly along, I turned my head round to look up the path and there was a light up there, quite a bright light, shining out in the blackout. I said to myself 'this won't do, I must go and have a look'.

I went up the footpath and what did I see? This little French polisher on his hand and knees - or one hand and knees - crawling along the footpath, feeling his way with his left hand against the wall and in his right hand holding a lit candle to see where he was going.

Well, obviously, I told him to

"Put that candle out!" So he put the candle out, and I told him to get on his way, so he stands up then and staggers away up the footpath.

I came back into Victoria Street, went on towards Temple Gate, where lo and behold Jock Copeland was put on the same duty again. We had a little chat - not very long, and I started to go back again towards Bristol Bridge.

When I came to the footpath I thought,

'H'm, let's see what has happened to him (the French polisher) if he's still about."

So I went up the footpath, turned around the corner in Rose Street and promptly fell over something. I looked down and there was chummy, fast asleep with his head rolled on his rolled up greatcoat. Once again,

"Come on mate, on your feet, get going."

I saw him to the end of Rose Street, he turned to the right and started towards Temple Bridge. I thought that's alright, if he goes that way A Division's just the other side of the bridge, he'll be off my patch.

So I let him go.

Anyway, I finished my patrol up to Bristol Bridge, across the road, came back again going a bit quicker this time as it was getting towards time to go off.

I suppose I arrived at the Temple Gate railway bridge or Temple Way, probably about five o'clock, it was just beginning to get light. I thought,

'Well, I wonder if chummy's disappeared? I'll take a stroll down Temple Way as far as the bridge.'

So I went steadily along the other side of the Great Western Railway Goods Yard, and suddenly I heard,

"H'rrrrrrr, H'rrrrrrr."

Standing there quietly I looked around. On the other side of Temple Way was a Barrage Balloon site.

It had been a bombed site and they had levelled it off a bit, there was the wagon parked, the balloon was down, alongside the wagon was the hut where the crew slept. I thought,

'Oh hallo, where's this noise coming from, sounds from over there.'

I crossed over Temple Way, climbed over the wire fence at the end of the balloon site and sure enough, there was chummy, fast asleep again. This time he had his head resting on the pulley that carried the cable coming from the balloon which was about six or seven feet above his head.

I thought,

'Well, I don't know." So I stood there and called,

"Anyone about?"

He didn't wake up, not a sign from the R.A.F. either. I am sure I could have picked that balloon up and carried it away in my pocket.

Dorry (glasses and moustache) holding back the crowds on VE Day 1945

Regular officers parade for inspection

 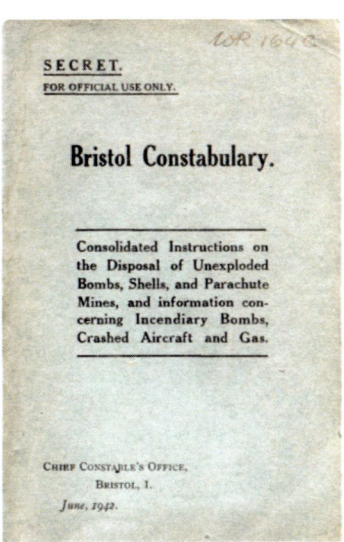

Two of the books that Dorry would have used (ASC collection)

Bristol officers taking part in gas drill. 1940 (ASC Collection)

ON THE
POLICE FRONT

Our Police in this war, Regular, War Reserve and Special Constabulary, have done a marvellous job. No blitz could scare them from their beat ; in the worst of fires with high explosives and incendiaries falling around them, they have carried on with their job, helping to rescue those trapped in the debris, bringing comfort and help to the homeless ; inspiring all by their cool, calm courage. These men are certainly doing a job comparable in its responsibility and danger with that of the other uniformed members of His Majesty's Forces ; and well may each policeman think as he goes on duty

"IT ALL DEPENDS ON ME"

Please pass this card on.

P.T.O.

PR message given out during the Bristol Blitz (ASC Collection)

Princes Street bridge after the bombing on 10 April 1941

The 'Dutch house' after the raid

Anyway, I thought something had to be done about this so I went up to the door of the hut, knocked on it, still nothing happened. So I tried the door handle, it was unlocked, I opened it and went in.

There were the rows of paliasses[2] down each side of the room, with the crew fast asleep. 'So!' I thought, this was getting too much of a good thing, I took my truncheon out, and gave it a really good bang on the floor – you ought to have seen the explosion.

All of them jumped out of their beds, the Corporal yelled,

"Turn out the guard!" and they all came round to see what had happened.

So I told them, they'd got a civilian asleep on the site, he could easily set fire to the balloon, I knew he'd got matches on him, where's the sentry?

So we went out to search for him and found him before long, on the lorry cleaning up the brass work on his engine. So I showed them where chummy was, we got him going again, sent off along Temple Way and he eventually disappeared over the bridge on to A Division. That was good enough for me, half past five, time to walk back to East Street.

Another incident which I recall and which I think happened around about this time, was really nothing directly connected with the war but more of a civilian police matter. One night I was again duty driver at East Street, the Sergeant came into our rest room and said,

"700 and you, and you" pointing to another two Special Constables.

"In the car with me. We're off to Temple Meads Station where there's been an accident."

We in due course arrived at Temple Meads where we were met in the main entrance hall by the Railway Police. Officers. They took us on to the main London departure platform and we walked along it in the direction of Temple Meads East signal box. Just before we left the end of the platform the Railway Police said to us.

"Now you chaps, you've got to be very careful, there's very little lighting here, and you must keep a good look out for approaching trains."

Sure enough the lighting was very poor, just some dim lights on very tall standards, which gave, well, just enough visibility to see where the rails were so you didn't fall over them.

They took us along the tracks to where the accident had occurred and we found that a foreman shunter had tripped over a rail just in front of a train, he finished up with his legs on one rail and his shoulders and neck on the other. The train had gone over him, and both his legs and his arms and head had been cut off.

The Railway Police had brought a stretcher with them and we had not the enjoyable task of picking up the pieces and putting them on a stretcher. Whilst we were doing this all the lights suddenly went out and left us in absolute pitch darkness. One of the railway men called out,

"Oh there it is then, 'purple up', wait for the sirens."

Well, I can assure you that I didn't enjoy the feeling being there, total darkness and trains passing by, very likely to be run over if you weren't extremely careful. I could well see how this poor chap had met his end.

After a minute or two the sirens sounded, and the guns started to fire. We carried on as best we could picking up the pieces, but there was still one bit missing and that was his head.

We had a good look round with our torches and we eventually found it some yards away where it had been thrown following the accident.

[1] *A thin straw mattress.*
[2] *Police Sergeant 97 Joseph Henry Copland. Born 1917, joined Bristol Constabulary 4 January 1939, retired 30 September 1967. Served 3 years 11 months in the Scots Guards. Recalled to the Army 1/12/1939. Returned to police duties 19/2/1941*

BLITZ

During this summer and autumn sporadic raids continued to be made and the sirens continued to be sounded by day and by night. As I have already said this was a very wearying time and one did not get very much unbroken rest.

In September however, things got even worse for me, personally. We normally had four engineers at Temple Back Power Station (*Dorry's day job*) and worked a four cycle shift of 42 hours per week.

Unfortunately during September one of my colleagues fell over a small low wall in the yard during an air raid and injured his head. It turned out later that he had displaced a vertebrae and he was off duty for a year or so. This reduced us to a compliment of three, and we had to cover the 168 hours a week by working 56 hours each. That was seven days a week, eight hours a day and no nights off. This extra burden was my undoing, as I will now relate.

I well remember going home one morning after doing duty at East Street Police Station all night. During the preceding week I had worked 56 hours at Temple Back and over 90 hours on duty at East Street[1]. I came up Colston Street in my car, at the top turned sharp left - a maneuver which one could do in those days, into Perry Road, with a view to turning up St Michaels Hill. I could remember getting as far as St Michaels Hill and after that everything was dark. I will continue to tell the story in the next installment.

Eventually I recovered consciousness to find myself being treated in the Casualty Department of the B.R.I. (Bristol Royal Infirmary).

According to witnesses, I must have fallen asleep at the wheel and turned right up St Michaels Hill immediately in front of an oncoming lorry. In the resulting crash, my car was destroyed, and I received fractured ribs, fractured skull, concussion and other bruises and scratches. Naturally, I was admitted to a ward in the hospital and I stayed for some three weeks or so, eventually being discharged on the 19 November to go home and continue my convalescence.

Within a few days life was to change most dramatically.

On Sunday the 25 November 1940, the sirens sounded for the 274th time at 6.15pm. As I was still on sick leave I didn't take any particular notice for a few moments - or should I say an hour or so - until looking out of the window I noticed that there were flares over the city, the guns were firing and it seemed as though Bristol was the target for that night.

It was soon quite obvious that this was going to be a most serious matter and I decided that even though I wasn't really well, I ought perhaps to get into uniform and see if I could do anything.

This I did and the next thing I can remember is being in Abbotsford Road, Redland, whilst incendiaries were coming down, and doing my best to extinguish them.

After some while I found myself going down St Michaels Hill towards the town, I went up Broad Street, to the junction of High Street and Wine Street and there, I shall never forget the sight, the whole area seemed to be engulfed in flames.

The Old Dutch House was on fire, Hones's in Wine Street was on fire, further premises were on fire down in Bridge Street, in High Street and everywhere seemed to be in flames.

However, I continued walking slowly down towards Bristol Bridge dodging the falling embers and bits of shrapnel and all sorts of odd things, when I got to Bristol Bridge, there were so many fire engines and hoses on the bridge that it was impossible to get to the other side.

As I wasn't really fit to do any hard work, I decided the only thing I could do was make my way back towards home and see if there were any other light jobs I could do.

One sideline, I shall never forget on that night, seeing the fire appliance from the Wellington Fire Brigade arrive in Bristol.

The old type of fire engine used in those days was fairly well known, it consisted of in effect, a large lorry with a bench seat across the front for the driver and senior officer, behind which was a box like structure with doors in the side containing the hoses, branches, keys, standpipes and other equipment for the Fire Brigades use. On top of this box rested the ladder fire escape which was a long ladder with two big wheels at one end, these wheels overhanging the end of the vehicle. The ladder resting along the top of the box and on to a bracket which was above the head of the driver and senior officer.

Along the side between the front and rear mudguards on each side was a running board and upon this the firemen stood while going to a fire, they held themselves in position by hooking their arms through the ladder and stood there facing each other.

This particular fire engine had come from Wellington, a distance of some 60 miles with no protection for the crew or the driver, or anybody, and had hung on there all the way up through that bitterly cold night.

When they eventually arrived in Bristol they were so frozen solid that they had to be helped off the fire engine and gently thawed out before they could do any duty.

I can't say that I was exactly frightened on that night, certainly not as much as I was on one or two other occasions later on. It was a novelty there was so much to do and so much happening that one really hadn't time to think about what was going on. But just to get on with the job in hand.

The awesome story of that night has frequently been told in other places, and I am afraid it is beyond me to better the descriptions already given. However, the 'All Clear' sounded about midnight and I carried upon my way.

The next day I can remember is being on C Division in Pembroke Road, Clifton, where there was a house on fire.

I reported to the Sergeant and was detailed to do point duty at the junction of Alma Road and Pembroke Road, to divert any traffic going towards the city down Alma Road as Pembroke Road was blocked by this fire and the fire appliances. By five o'clock in the morning I was beginning to feel the strain and I obtained permission to go home and thus finished my first baptism of fire in the major blitz of Bristol.

[1] *If Dorry's recollections are accurate then he had only a total of 22 non-working hours in seven days.*

The Aftermath of Bombing

As I did not live on my Police Division, I often used to find myself in strange places during air raids.

Talking of the Pembroke Road area *(previous chapter)*, reminds me of one night, I've no idea when it was, I was coming up Triangle West towards Queens Road just about opposite where Maggs Furniture Store used to be.

There was a raid in progress, I was wearing my tin hat needless to say and a certain amount of shrapnel was falling down from the sky.

I saw on the other side of Queens Road a soldier and a girl friend walking along, neither of them with any tin hat or anything on. They were going slowly close into the buildings, I shouted out to them to get under cover in the Air Raid Shelter in Queens Avenue, but they didn't take any particular notice.

So I walked smartly across the road towards them intending to give them a telling off, when I heard the whistle of a bomb coming down.

I threw myself at them and the three of us finished on the pavement. I just had time to look up towards the Victoria

Rooms when the bomb - luckily a small one - landed near the fountains outside.

It is the only time I saw a bomb explode, I saw the actual flash and luckily didn't get any injury. Anyway, that convinced these two silly people that they'd better do something about it so they ran very quickly round the corner and went into the Air Raid Shelter.

I reported in on the police telephone pillar on the corner of Queens Avenue and Whiteladies Road to the effect that this bomb had fallen outside the Victoria Rooms, no damage visible and I was told to stay there and do anything necessary.

A few minutes later a Warden came up to me and said,

"Excuse me officer, but something seems to have happened at the side of Beacon House."

I said, "Oh, what's that?"

"Well" he said, "There's a hole in the wall. You'd better go and have a look."

So I went along to have a look, he didn't come with me, and there in the side of Beacon House, opposite the entrance to the cinema (*The Embassy*), sure enough there was a hole in the wall, quite a big one. I suppose it was two or three feet wide and perhaps six feet high and bricks had been knocked out.

I gingerly tiptoed forward, shone my torch, down into this hole and what did I see, but about ten feet below ground level the fins of a bomb, something like three to four feet across, quite a large one.

I thought,

'Oh Lord, here's an unexploded bomb known as a UXB.'

Back to the police pillar quickly, rang into Redland and said,

"There's a large, about 500lbs UXB in the side of Beacon House."

I was then told that reinforcements would be sent down immediately, but that I should start evacuating all the premises in Queens Avenue. That is a lot of houses going into Woodland Road, the Air Raid Shelters, Beacon House itself, get any firewatchers out and generally start clearing the place up.

Before long the Sergeant arrived with a squad of Specials and we all set to getting everybody away. The bomb did not go off before it was removed but it turned out that it was an oil bomb ready to start a major fire.

As I no longer had a car, I managed to purchase a secondhand bicycle and much of my energy for the next six months or so was spent in cycling between home and East Street and back again. Sometimes two or three times in a single night.

Also life became more or less one round of duty of one sort or another.

My normal dress at this time became uniform trousers and a civilian jacket of some sort. Wherever I went I carried a uniform mackintosh (*raincoat*) and steel helmet and respirator, thus if the sirens sounded, wherever I was I put on my mackintosh, tin hat, brought my respirator to the ready position and I was then able to go on to the streets and start duty.

If there was a pillar anywhere near, I used to ring in, but if not, I just went out onto the road to do what I could to see people got safely to a shelter or to deal with any incidents which might occur.

It was about this time that after three nights of duty I was extremely tired and so on the fourth night I went to bed in the early evening hoping to get a good night's rest.

I soon went off to sleep but about ten o'clock the sirens sounded and although they woke me up, I was so dog tired, I really could not bring myself to get out of bed and report to duty.

I lay there for a few minutes half awake, half asleep when suddenly there was a whistling sound, I dived on to the floor by the side of the bed and there was an enormous bang, it didn't seem very far away.

"Oh well," I thought, "this is it."

I got my uniform on, went out, and was soon informed that a bomb had fallen on a house in Ravenswood Road at the back of the road where I lived. *(Cotham/Redland area of Bristol.)*

I went down there and found a crowd of local people standing outside this house which had been almost demolished to ground level.

There were no official wardens or rescue people about, but I was told that there were three old ladies who lived in the house and that they hadn't been seen since the bomb fell. They usually slept in the basement cellars.

Looking at the front of the house there was a bay window and beneath that at pretty much ground level, was an opening protected by a grille of iron bars. They told me that this led into the cellars. I had a look at it and it looked as if it had been shaken up quite a bit so I got my trusty truncheon out and started work on the stone work and the iron bars with the truncheon.

When I left the force in 1977 I still had the same truncheon and it still carried the scars from that war time experience.

Anyway, I eventually managed to get a way into the cellar so I went down and found that the cellar floor was something like four feet below ground level. It was covered in rubble, I shone my torch round making my way to the back and shouted out,

"Anybody about?" and I heard one or two feeble female voices saying,

"Yes, over here."

So I went through the doorway towards the back of the house and underneath the stairs which had fallen down I saw three figures, lying on blankets. There were my three old ladies covered in dust, and although the top half of their bodies were clear, their feet were trapped underneath some rubble, nothing very heavy, just ordinary bits of bricks and what have you.

So I started scrabbling about around trying to get their legs free, and one of them looked up at me and said,

"It's no good looking down there for me young man. You won't find any pieces of me down there."

So I looked at her a bit peculiarly, she said "Try further up."

So I tried further up and eventually got her out. I then followed up by getting the other two old ladies out.

Soon some people came in through into the cellar to help me and we got them all out into the street.

It was not until then that I realised that the first lady I had been trying to get out was a dwarf and I had been scrabbling about somewhere well beyond her feet.

NEW CARS AND TIN HATS

I think the next incident to relate is Prince's Wharf. I am not quite sure of the date but I think it was on the night of the 3rd and 4th January 1941[1].

At that time the Fire Brigade was named G Division of the Bristol Constabulary, and of course we came under the orders of their officers. I found myself on the beat eventually in Wapping Road at the back of Prince's Wharf when a Fire Inspector came up to me and said,

"700 take over that branch from those two firemen, they'll have to go and have a rest."

This I promptly did, only to find that the branch in question was a one inch branch fed off the fire float 'Pyronaut'.[2]

Now this Fire Float gave water at a higher pressure than the ordinary fire appliances and the branch was about as much as one man could hold, normally two men were put on it.

Anyhow I took over the branch, tucked it under my arm in the approved manner and stood there letting the water play on the flames. It was as much as I could do to hold it.

With that, these bombs started coming down all around. I saw railway lines in the distance begin to curl up into the air, and I was rather scared. I daren't let go of the branch however, because if I did, well you know what happens with a garden hose with the pressure on it, it will come around, whip round smartly and hit you on the head or something and of course this was a big hose with a very high pressure on it.

So I stood there quivering in my boots holding this hose and hoping that nothing landed too near. The fire which I was dealing with was quite a spectacular one as the building in question was the Guinness shed which was used for storing large quantities of Guinness and also wines and spirits. Of course the spirits caught fire, added fuel to the blaze and it was a really good one.

I have previously mention Inspector Basil Richardson, who besides his dignified manner, had a reputation for being completely unflappable, cool and calm under any circumstances. This was born out by an incident which occurred about this time, I think on the 17th January.

I was in the Charge Office in East Street Station, talking to the Sergeant or somebody else when the door opened and in walks Basil Richardson covered in dust and looking very weary indeed.

He marches smartly up to the counter, salutes the Superintendent and says,

"Sir." and the Superintendent said

"What the devil have you been up to Basil?" and he says,

"I regret sir, that I shall have to requisition a new car for this Division."

The Superintendent said,

"What the dickens is going on?"

It appears that during the night, bombs had been falling in Bedminster one of which had landed in Bedminster Road, near to the Parsons Street Schools and Basil Richardson who was the duty Inspector went out to visit the incident.

He parked his car in Bedminster Road some little distance away and walked up to the incident officer who saluted him smartly and said,

"All correct, Sir." And Basil said,

"Well, how are things going?" and they had a chat for a few moments. Then the incident officer - who was a Sergeant - looked up and said,

"Excuse me Sir, is that your car just parked down the road there?"

"Yes, and what about it?"

"Well Sir, you've parked it alongside an unexploded bomb."

At that moment the bomb went off and blew the car to smithereens. Basil looks at the Sergeant and said,

"That was most unfortunate Sergeant, I shall have to walk back to East Street." And he turned round and calmly walked back into the station.

Talking of personal matters for a moment, once the raids had really started, in December 1940, we found at Temple Back

Power Station that the night shift engineer had great difficulty in getting to the station owing to the raids. This meant of course, that the engineer on evenings had to stay on all night and sometimes work something like an 18 hour shift.

We therefore decided to alter our working arrangements. We divided the day into two, a day shift and a night shift.

The day shift was from 9.00 am to 5.00 pm and we then worked a 16 hour night from 5.00 pm to 9.00 am. Our colleague was still sick and we went on three cycles, so we worked alternate nights for a fortnight then a week of days, then back on to nights again.

Working alternate nights was not very good for ones living conditions, digestion and so on and so I arranged to do my normal police duty on alternate nights during the two weeks I was on nights at Temple Back, this enabled me to have every day in bed and stay up every night. A much better arrangement.

At the same time the Regular and War Reserve Constables were put on extra duty doing their normal eight hour tour and also have to do four hours on stand-by in the Station, if there were no air raid on.

The early turn came on at two o'clock in the morning, stayed until six and then went out and did their normal duty until two o'clock. The late turn came on at two o'clock, did their police duty until ten and then stayed on stand-by until twelve o'clock in the morning. (That is to say if there were no raids on and if they were not required to carry on for air raid purposes. The night shift were not given any extra stand-by duty but it was not very often that they managed to get away at six in the morning as they should have done. They were usually busy clearing up after an air raid.

Special Constables likewise were put on a stand-by and we spent quite a lot of time in the station. This was when I learnt to play snooker and 'Pontoon' and indulge in similar amusements. Refreshments were laid on and we used to have a lot of time in the War Inspectors office playing cards and eating cheese and pickle sandwiches and multitudinous gallons of tea.

Anyhow, when there was a raid on they used to send us out in cars, four to a car, so that we should not all be congregated in one place if a bomb should fall on East Street Station.

We would go out into the Division and ring in from a pillar and we would then be sent to a particular incident, and when that was cleared and we could be spared we would ring on the nearest pillar at least every ten minutes, and if a bomb fell where we were, we would report it and then go along and deal with the incident.

On one such occasion we went up from East Street, along West Street out towards the Avonleigh Road area. We got to Chessel Street, where there was a police pillar and we laid up there.

Bombs started to fall so we rang in on the pillar and asked for instructions and we were told that a bomb had fallen in Avonleigh Road alongside the Air Raid Shelter. An incident had been dealt with by the A.R.P. Services *(Air Raid Precautions)* but we were told to go along and have a look and see if there was anything we could do.

I went along in the car and was detailed to go and have a look in the shelter and see that everything was alright.

I went in to the shelter and there were the usual benches along the side walls with about half a dozen people sitting on the benches. They were remarkably still and quiet, and I went up to the first one, and she was dead. I went along to the others and found that all six of them had been killed.

There was not a mark on them, they had died from blast effect. The A.R.P. services were too busy to deal with them at the time and they were left in the shelter until after the raid had finished and they could be removed to the mortuary.

On another night I was sent out with a Regular Constable to patrol along Clarence Road towards Temple Meads Station. No bombs were falling in our area although other parts of the city were having a bit of a pasting.

We were rather scared, I must admit, and we were walking along arm in arm to keep up our courage. We got to the corner of Langton Street and Clarence Road and suddenly all the guns stopped firing and everything fell quiet. Enemy aircraft were still about but nothing much was falling down.

As we stepped off the kerb at the corner of Langton Street, there was an almighty bang quite close by, the Constable and I let out one yell and fell on our faces flat in the roadway.

Bang. Bang. Bang!

We lay there for a bit wondering what was going on and eventually plucked up the courage to lift our heads and have a look. About a hundred yards away up Langton Street was a mobile anti-aircraft gun, firing away at the enemy and the crew roaring their heads off with laughter at the sight of two hefty policemen lying flat on their faces in the middle of the road.

Another problem which we encountered at this time was the steel helmet. Owing to the frequency of air raid alerts we were instructed to wear steel helmets at all times instead of the usual caps. The helmet in those days was nothing like the modern plastic ones, but was a proper steel helmet and after eight hours carrying this around on your head your neck soon began to ache.

Talking of helmets. One night I was in East Street Station having a chat to the people there, including the Superintendent, who had rather a distorted sense of humour.

Suddenly I felt a terrific blow on my head which brought me down to my knees. When I stood up again there was the Superintendent, grinning all over his face with his truncheon in his hand.

"I've always wondered if these steel helmets were really any good," he said.

I took my helmet off and there was a dent all the way up one side of it where he had hit me on the head with his truncheon. My helmet for the rest of the war carried this honourable battle scar.

I should have mentioned another incident which occurred on the night we went out to Avonleigh Road air raid shelter. We went from East Street Station up West Street to Chessel Street pillar, where we telephoned in and were told to go to this shelter in Avonleigh Road.

Having completed our job there, we went back to the pillar, rang in and were told to return to the Station. I suppose we hadn't been out much more than an hour or so. Anyway, we turned the car back to East Street.

We were going nicely along West Street at a reasonable pace and suddenly the front seat passenger called out,

"Look out!"

The driver slammed his brakes on and we came to a sudden halt. It appeared that while we were away a bomb had fallen right in the middle of West Street and we were on the edge of a bomb crater about 15 feet deep and extending across most of the carriage way. Life certainly could be exciting at times.

---

[1] *On 3rd January 1941 Bristol was subjected a 12 hour sustained bombing attack which was to become the longest of the war. The area targeted was the docks area around Prince's Wharf and the railway network.*

[2] *Pyronaut can still be seen, fully restored and docked alongside the 'M Shed' in Bristol'*

A LONG TOUR

Now we come to the heaviest raid on Bristol and probably the longest turn of duty I have ever done.

On Maundy Thursday, 10 April 1941 I was on night shift at Temple Back Power Station and I came off duty at nine o'clock on Friday morning, not expecting to see the station again until five o'clock on the Saturday. How wrong was I!

I got home about ten o'clock on Good Friday morning, went to bed, had a good sleep and got up about seven o'clock in the evening to have my breakfast. When I had finished eating I sat down in an armchair to take my ease before going on duty at East Street.

Unfortunately I hadn't been in my chair very long when the sirens sounded.

So, I got into my uniform, got onto my bicycle and set off to make my way across the city to Bedminster. I got as far as the bottom of St Michaels hill and it was now obvious that Bristol was the target for tonight, with flares and bombs dropping all over the city.

At the top of Colston Street I saw a long motor car coming up Maudlin Street, making its precarious way through the falling debris so I stepped out to stop it. As I approached the driver to advise him to take shelter, he exited the vehicle and to my surprise it was Ceddie Blackett one of the engineers I worked with at the Power Station.

Ceddie explained that our Colston Avenue offices were on fire and asked for my assistance. I decided that the police could wait for a while and I went along to Colston Avenue where I found that the top floors of the building were well alight.

Luckily, the mains maps and records were stored in an alleged fire proof brick and concrete room which had been built in the yard at the back of the premises.

The sole fire appliance in attendance obviously would not control the fire and it seemed likely that the building would collapse at any moment.

We made a decision that we needed to get the indispensable maps out of the store to a place of safety. By this time, several members of staff had arrived on the scene so a human chain was formed to carry the documents from the yard to the cars outside.

I found myself in the map room pulling maps off the racks, bundling them up and throwing them to the Chief Engineer and General Manager[1].

We had just about cleared the lot when the Fire Brigade ordered us from the yard due to the heavy debris that was falling from the collapsing building.

Within a few minutes we had finished the job and most thankfully we ran out of the yard to the safer road outside.

Back onto my trusty bicycle again I continued the journey to Bedminster, frequently having to jump off the bike and take cover when I heard a bomb whistling down near at hand.

Eventually I made it and reported for duty. You can imagine my delight when, alongside War Reserve Constable 106B I was detailed for duty at Temple Back Power Station! Oh well!

106 and I set off with instructions that we would be relieved at two in the morning to enable us to return to Bedminster for 'refreshments' (as the meal break was called).

We duly arrived at Temple Back having met the late tour guide on the way whilst the raid was still in progress. It was not quite as heavy as it had been and we heartily hoped that it might end soon.

At seven minutes to midnight our hopes were realised and the 'All Clear' was sounded.

The whole Power Station had a cable basement beneath it and this had been adapted as a very strong Air Raid Shelter for the use of the power station staff. At night this basement was also used by the inmates of Dr Whites Almshouses which were situated in Temple Street opposite.

Incidentally, we were greatly indebted to the old ladies from the almshouses who spent the raids placidly knitting skull-caps for us to wear under our steel helmets which served as protection from the icy weather.

106 and I thought we would take the opportunity to have a look around the power station and make sure that all was well.

We found our guests settled down in the basement, the fire watchers on duty, the charge engineer in his office and the switchboard attendant and telephonists at their posts, so we commenced our patrol around the boundary.

The bombing had ceased and the only sounds to be heard were the throbbing of fire pumps, the crash of falling buildings and the roar of the many fires still blazing.

Our moment of peace was not to last very long however, as at three minutes past twelve the switchboard attendant poked his head out of one of the station windows and said,

"Purple up."

Three minutes later the sirens sounded and we were back in air raid conditions again.

A quiet hour or so passed but the lull ended at one o'clock in the morning when we heard the 'raiders overhead' buzzer sounding in the power station. The 'muck' then started to fall in very great numbers.

At about quarter to two the raid was at its height and there was indeed a lot of heavy bombing going on. I consulted with my colleague and we went into the power station and ordered all the staff there to go to the shelter.

Having seen this order carried out I told 106 that I would telephone to our Sergeant at East Street Police Station to tell him that we would not be coming in for refreshments as the raid was much too heavy to go through the streets.

I advised him to get under cover while we could but he said, "No", his duty was outside the building, and the most he would do was stand at the top of the steps leading from the station yard into the basement taking some slight shelter from the doorway.

I went into the telephone exchange inside the power station to speak to Bedminster and had just time to pass my message to the Sergeant when there was an almighty bang outside. The Sergeant said,

"Blimey that was not far away" and the phone went dead.

The running machine that was on load at the time started to slow down, showing that once again we had lost our incoming high voltage electricity supply. This was then followed by the most awful sound I have ever heard, as though the whole building was collapsing.

I am not ashamed to confess that I dived under the telephonists table and covered my head with my hands thinking that my end had come at last.

After a minute or two the noise subsided, I plucked up my courage to come out from under the table, opened the door to the telephone room and peeped out into the engine room.

What a sight met my eyes. The engine room had a glass roof on to which had fallen tone of debris and the machines were covered in rubble and broken glass. This was the cause of the noise I had heard.

I went out into the yard and the first things I saw were huge blocks of stone lying all over the yard and a six foot length of tram rail embedded in the tarmac.

I called out to my colleague and receiving no reply was greatly afraid that he must have been killed or seriously injured. After a few more calls I heard a feeble reply from the basement and heard him crawling up the steps from the basement where he had been blown by the explosion. He had been blown backwards down the entire flight of twelve stairs but he was only bruised.

Naturally we decided that there must have been a 'Big 'Un' falling nearby so we set out to have a look.

106 went along Temple Back towards Temple Way while I turned in the other direction and went along towards Bath Street. I looked around, couldn't see any buildings missing or any fires but there was any amount of debris.

I turned my head to look across St Philips Bridge towards Old Market and my eyes nearly popped out. No bridge, only the remains of the carriageway drooping into the floating harbour supported by a tangle of electric cables.

At this moment I heard the bell of a fire engine approaching from Old Market Street, so I ran up to the edge of the broken bridge waving my torch, blowing my whistle and shouting.

Still the fire engine came on.

Luckily the driver saw the missing bridge just in time to skid to a stop on the brink – to my great relief as I don't like cold water and was not looking forward to having to dive to the rescue.

I went back to the power station to report the matter to Bedminster Incident control but I found I couldn't get through. Instead, I reported it to the Central Division and told them of the demise of St Philips Bridge.

I later found out that the bomb that had demolished the bridge was one of a stick of three, the last of which had fallen on Redcliffe Hill demolishing an underground electricity sub-station and severing the telephone cables between Central and Bedminster Telephone exchanges.

Having got matters under control I went outside to find 106 and met him coming from Temple Way. He said,

"I couldn't find anything amiss, no fires, all the buildings still there." So I said,

"Come and see what I've found" and I took him along to Bath Street.

One often hears the expression, 'and his mouth fell open' but I have never before seen it actually happen.

The time would now be round about half past two or quarter to three and the raid had eased off a bit so we thought we would go and see how the staff at the Tramways Power Station situated on the other side of Bath street were getting on.

When we arrived at the building we went into the engine room which was on the ground floor, only to find the engineers and switchboard attended in a very distressed state with streaming eyes and coughing their heads off. Some bomb fragments had pierced the refrigerator cooling tubes of the Avon Cold Stores on the other side of the harbour and the slight breeze was blowing ammonia gas through the broken glass straight into the powers station.

A small side line, regarding the Bristol Tramways. By that time there had been so much damage to the tram tracks that all the routes had been abandoned except those to Kingswood and Hanham from Old Market Street.

The company had applied to the Ministry of Transport for permission to close these routes also and replace them with buses. On Easter Saturday the Ministry's Inspector was due in Bristol to hold an enquiry into the application and to see if permission could be granted for a change from trams to buses. The demolition of St Philips Bridge had severed the Tramway Company's cables to Kingswood and Hanham, effectively separating the remaining trams from their source of power.

The Inspectors comment when he arrived was,

"It would seem that my enquiry is somewhat superfluous and permission to close is granted!" This I think must have been one of the shortest Government Enquiries on record.

There was not much left for us to do in the area so 106 and I commenced our patrol around the station once more. The 'All Clear' was eventually sounded at 03.52 hours that morning and thus ended the last of the saturation raids on Bristol.

We stayed at out post until shortly before six o'clock when we set off towards East Street to meet our reliefs on the way. In due course we arrived at the station and then had our very belated meal.

I was asked if I could stay on a little longer as they were very busy on Bedminster Division and I said that I could stay for another few hours.

I'm not quite certain if this was the occasion, but I think it was anyway so we'll assume that this was so.

I was then sent round to Willway Street, an area at the back of East Street between there and the main railway line. During the night the fire watchers had seen some parachutes coming down and they assumed that they were being invaded.

They called out to their neighbours to come out and catch the 'Jerries' and they watched this parachute coming towards them. Unfortunately it was not a soldier that was hanging beneath the parachute but a huge landmine.

By the time the people realised this was so, it was too late for them to do anything about it. The landmine exploded upon contact with the ground killing all the people who were in the open nearby and demolishing a couple of streets and a hundred or so small houses.

This I think was the worst incident that we had on our division, I spent a couple of hours or so at Willway Street doing what I could to help. Digging people out, looking after those who had been killed and those who had lost their relatives.

I then went back to East Street Station to report that there wasn't very much more I could do but I was immediately told to get out to the South side of Bedminster Bridge and take up a traffic point there.

An unexploded bomb had been found on the east side of Bristol and the bomb disposal squad had been trying to defuse it. Although the bomb was liable to go off at any moment it was decided that the only thing to do was to take it to the bomb cemetery in Ashton Court.

Its route where I was concerned was to come along York Road, cross over East Street Bedminster, and to disappear down Coronation Road. I was told to get out there, take up the point, and stop all traffic coming up East Street and off Bedminster Bridge as soon as I had any signs of this convoy approaching.

I supposed I'd been there about quarter of an hour or twenty minutes when I heard the sound of bells and sirens in the background and the convoy came along. It was headed by a police car and then came a jeep carrying the bomb disposal squad and behind this a lorry with the bomb loaded on top.

They were going like the clappers, I haven't seen anyone go so fast for a long time, and oh boy was I thankful when they got past my point and disappeared down Coronation Road safely.

We heard in the end that they had indeed got down to the bomb cemetery and there the bomb disposal unit had eventually blown the bomb up.

About midday I eventually signed off duty having been on for over 16 hours and went back home to get what little sleep I could before I went on shift again at the power station at five o'clock that afternoon.

[1] *Mr. A J Newman known by the staff as 'Uncle Arthur'*
[2] *Records indicate that 106B was Police Constable Raymond March. Joined 9 June 1937 and left 3 April 1946*

UXB AND W.A.P.C.

For those that are interested in statistics it may be worth mentioning that during this raid, Bristol's 68 heavy guns fired a total of 5,781 rounds of 3.7 inch and 954 rounds of 3 inch ammunition.

This gives a firing rate of approximately one round every three and a half seconds on average for the complete barrage.

It is no wonder that a lot of muck was falling from the sky. Not only the bombs coming down in one piece but all sorts of pieces of shrapnel of various sizes from the anti-aircraft shells which had exploded far up in the sky.

Talking of unexploded bombs, one night when we had been sent to the Southville area we got onto a police pillar to ring into the station to say that we had finished and that we were returning.

Upon doing this we were told quite emphatically that under no circumstances were we to return to the station but we were to go to the Wardens Post or some other suitable place where there was a telephone, ring into the station giving the telephone number and then stay on standby until further notice.

We later found out that an unexploded bomb had fallen in a tyre warehouse immediately adjoining the Police Station just on the other side of the wall at the side of our telephone exchange.

Although this bomb had not exploded and was likely to go off, the girl telephonists who were on duty in the telephone exchange that night, refused to leave their posts but all other personnel were evacuated from the station. They are to be highly commended for their courage and devotion to duty in staying there dealing coolly and calmly with all telephone calls coming into the division, despite the fact that they knew that at any moment they might be blown to pieces.

Another rather amusing incident concerned with our girls, arose during one night.

For some time, since the beginning of the war, there had been female staff in the Police Force, some of them were civilians and some had joined the Women's Auxiliary Police Corps *(W.A.R.P)*. The Corps were all in uniform but not sworn in as constables.

Partly through the war it was decided that they should be sworn in and become regular Women Police Officers.

We had, at that time in East Street Station, a rather objectionable character, a regular constable reaching the end of his service, who was rather prone to use bad language and was a surly type altogether.

One night he was jeering at these Policewomen and said,

"Hmm, what do you think you would do if you had to bring in a drunken navvy?"

One of the girls calmly said,

"Well I should arrest him and bring him in."

"Hmm, you and who else?" stated the constable.

"No, I could do it. I would bring him in." She said.

With that the constable squared up to her and pretended to be fighting with her and the next moment he was flat on his back on the floor of the Charge Office.

The girls had all been taught self defence and she easily overcame him and after he just crawled away quietly into a corner of the station and we had no further trouble with him during the whole of the war.

Although the Good Friday raid marked the last of the big raids on Bristol the sirens were to sound another 200 times before the raids were completely finished. Many of these siren calls actually had no bombing and it was a waste of my time going down to East Street every time they sounded.

It was therefore agreed that I should report to the Homoeopathic Hospital which is situated at the end of the road where I live, in order to do duty there.

This hospital was an evacuation hospital to receive casualties after an air raid and the duty I had to do was to be prepared to open up a traffic point and see that the ambulance got a clear run into the hospital.

On two occasions enemy planes came over the city at a low altitude and did some shooting up of the population. Of course I managed to get involved in one of them.

One fine Sunday afternoon in the summer of 1941, I was taking a walk with a friend on the Downs and we were at the time at the junction of Camp Road and Percival Road in Clifton.

Suddenly we heard the sound of an aircraft approaching firing its guns. We threw ourselves down against the wall and hoped for the best. Sure enough, some of the shells hit the wall not very far from us but we were not injured.

Just after this had finished the sirens sounded and of course by that time the plane had gone well on its way back to Germany.

AFTERTHOUGHTS

That just about concludes all the memories I can recall where I was involved with the war as a Special Constable but there is one other incident that is worthy of mention.

It happened on the 25 September 1940 before the main raids had started.

By that time the Civil Defence organization in factories included roof spotting, that is to say a member of staff was sent up on to the roof with binoculars in order to detect any aircraft likely to cause trouble over the factory.

On the day which I have mentioned I was on day shift at the power station and the sirens sounded at about half past eleven in the morning. My switchboard attendant who was on duty that day was sent up on to the roof as a roof-spotter.

To do this, he had to go out through one of the windows of my office where he could get on to the roof down to the far end of the building where his post was. Not long after the sirens had sounded he came running down the roof and said, "one or two enemy aircraft approaching."

I immediately sounded the 'Raiders overhead' signal on the buzzer and he went back to his post.

He then came back and said,

"about a dozen or so coming over" and once more returned to his post.

Then I heard him rushing down the roof at very high speed and he more or less fell through the window into the office and said,

"there's thousands of the bastards up there."

This was the occasion of the daylight raid on the Bristol Airplane Co at Filton. In 45 terror filled seconds, 57 planes dropped 168 bombs on the factory and about 70 people were killed.

Although the raid was of such short duration considerable damage was still caused.

Two days later the Germans came over again with the same intention at about 11.30 in the morning. A force of about nine bombers accompanied by fighters came over the city but a squadron of Hurricanes was waiting for them. Anti-aircraft guns were in action as well and the formation was dispersed before it could reach its target.

Regardless of the danger, crowds of people came out on to the streets to watch the dog fights taking place in the sky.

That really ends my memories of my time as a Special Constable during the war, but there were two other little items which I should have mentioned when I was talking about training.

Besides having to salute whenever one met an officer there were two other occasions when this was necessary. The first was if one saw the Lord Mayor approaching in his car you had to come to attention, face the carriageway and salute him as he went by.

The second one was a funeral. If you saw a funeral coming, you again had to stand to attention, face the carriageway and salute the hearse as it passed.

On 15 May 1944 the last entry in the official record in the Battle of Bristol was made. This was the last scene in the last act in a drama that lasted almost four years. Set in a wounded city which had bravely lived up to a proud and distinguished past, its players humble citizens whose gallantry and fortitude will be an example for all time.

On this night ten high explosives fell, weighing a combined 13,000 pounds. Two were dropped in Kingsweston Lane, killing a Serviceman on a searchlight site and he was the only casualty in this final raid.

In Bedminster, three bombs descended near St Peter's Rise and Gifford's Hill damaging several houses on both sides of the city boundary and the remaining five bombs fell in the Abbots Leigh area, the responsibility of Somerset Constabulary.

At seven minutes past three in the morning the 'raiders passed' was sounded, the German bombers turned tail for home, and they never came back. Bristol's ordeal was over.

Between the 25 June 1940 when the alert was first sounded the sirens had given their warning no less than 563 times. The war in Europe ended on the 8 May 1945 and this brought to a close my time as a Special Constable on Wartime – but not my time in the Special Constabulary.

What a relief it was after that day to be able to parade on duty and to walk the streets without carrying the extra weight of a tin helmet and respirator!

Looking Back

Looking back on those wartime years Although I witnessed many scenes of tragedy and terror there were good times, we had some fun now and then and the camaraderie of the Police Force was enormous.

Soon after the war the Special Constabulary was stood down from its war time status and many of its men resigned.

Many more of us however, stayed on and continued to do police duties under peacetime conditions. We were given all sorts of jobs to do and gained quite a wide experience of things.

I personally dealt with suicides, both attempted and successful, sudden death, a suspected murder which turned out be an accident death and more. Besides the usual domestic disputes, disturbances, break and entries and similar things as that we also had to deal with the fights between various gangs of youths during the 'Teddy Boy' periods, several battles were held on our Division.

We also used to do football duty at the Bristol City ground taking crowd control, point duty and parking regulations.

On Fridays and Saturdays we used to do duty from about 6pm to 2am to assist the regular force in looking after the drunks and various occurrences which used to happen on those evenings.

In the summer of 1945 I purchased another car, a very ancient Wolseley Hornet and when I went on duty I was allowed to use it – providing it was at my own expense. I well remember the first night this happened.

I was detailed by Inspector Ashley to go and do duty on the Hartcliffe housing site which was then being built.

This would be some two or three miles from the station and there was a long and weary walk or cycle ride up to the estate, do four hours patrolling and then walk or cycle back to East Street. He was pulling my leg and said,

"Well what can we give you to do this evening 700? I think we'll send you up to Hartcliffe."

I said "Oh aye, you want to give me a bit of exercise do you sir? I'll go up there if I can take my car with me."

He said, "That's not a bad idea. Look, I'll detail a regular to go with you and the two of you can go up to Hartcliffe and see what you can find. We have been having a lot of thefts of building materials up there recently."

So, this young regular and myself set off in the car up to Hartcliffe. We hadn't been up there very long when driving down Cutler Road we saw a chap walking along pushing a perambulator. We thought this looked a little bit odd in the evening so we stopped to have a chat with him. When we looked inside the pram, lo and behold it was full of bricks!

"Oh ah, where did you get those from?"

"Well," he said, "I'm taking them home to build a garden path."

We told him that he was being arrested for the theft of bricks, put him and the bricks in the car and half an hour after leaving the station, we were back there again with our first prisoner.

This idea had been so successful that it became quite a regular thing for us to go out and look for thieves on the ground.

Life carried on this fashion until in 1968 I was appointed Deputy Commandant of the Division and later in February 1971 was appointed Divisional Commandant.

I remained in this post until I retired on 31 December 1977 after nearly 39 years' service."

J.W. Dorrinton

Appendix A

The letter on this page was received by Chief Constable Ronald Broome in 1989.

XXXXXXXX
XXXXXXXX
XXXXXXXX

10th April 1989

R. Broome, Esq., O.B.E.
Chief Constable
Avon & Somerset Constabulary
HEADQUARTERS

Dear Mr. Broome,

I have recently completed recording my reminiscences as a war-time Special Constable, and thought you might like to have a copy.

It might be suitable for inclusion in the Force Museum, and perhaps, Newsbeat might find an extract or two to be of interest.

Yours sincerely,

J.W.Dorrinton

'Our Wilf'

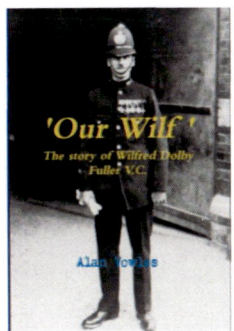

'Wilfred Dolby Fuller V.C. was a hero of his time. A son, a husband, a father, a miner, a Grenadier Guard and a Police Officer.

Never previously published as a full story, Wilfred's biography is a tale of supreme gallantry and hardship following him from his time in the 'pits' to his untimely end and beyond.

Share with Wilfred his surprise at winning the Victoria Cross after his brave actions at the battle of Neuve Chapelle and the public adoration that he experienced on his homecoming. Follow him through his career as a 'Bobby on the beat' in the 1920s and 30s, before reading of his legacy which stretches from Mansfield to Somerset.

Using previously unpublished records and photographs from the archives of Avon and Somerset Constabulary with assistance from the Guards Museum in London, this is a unique insight into a man whose sacrifice will always be remembered'

The book, with a forward by the Chief Constable of Avon and Somerset Constabulary, Andy Marsh and the Lt Colonel Commanding First Battalion Grenadier Guards is available now.

*All proceeds to Avon and Somerset Police History Group

When the whistle stops

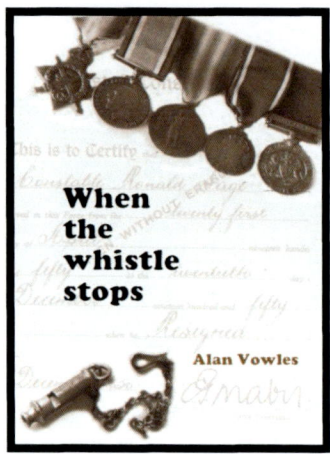

'When the whistle stops' is the first collection of biographies, stories, facts and photos produced as a result of two years exploring the dusty old boxes and long forgotten files that make up the history of Avon and Somerset Constabulary.

Supported by 83 photographs and drawings - many of which have never been published before – you will find stories of bravery, bereavement, humour, intrigue and love. With direct quotes from original statements and old handwritten poems about life on the beat this is a novel collection this is a 'must have' for anyone with an interest in history, policing or great true stories.

With stories dating from 1836 to the 1970's there is something for everyone in what is a celebration of the rich history of policing in the West Country.

*All proceeds to Avon and Somerset Police History Group